Knowledge

Management

Written by Nicholas Aitalegbe

In association with

Knowledge Management

Published in London by Peaches Publications, 2017.
www.peachespublications.com

British Library Cataloguing in Publication Data: A catalogue record for this book is available from the British Library.

Front cover image courtesy of Pixabay

ISBN: 978-0-244-60661-9

Book cover design: Nicholas Aitalegbe
Typesetter: Winsome Duncan.

Contents

Dedication

To my late father, Chief Jonah Oye Aitalegbe, who has inspired me to push on both while alive and even in death, he remains my ultimate role model for the amount of data and information he kept and managed in his lifetime.

To my loving and supportive wife, Nnennaya Annabel, who never stopped critiquing this work from start to finish, in such a loving way that I simply enjoy.

To my children, Felicity Omomeda, Joyce Omokeme, Toby Ekemayo and Joanne Aruemike; whom I love so much and will always do.

To my CRID family, clients and friends; for their steadfastness and support.
Without them, this book would have been impossible to complete.

Dedication

Acknowledgements

This work would not have been possible without the support of the team at CRID, especially my fellow Regional Directors for Caribbean, Michael Baptist and Regional Director for Asia Pacific, Jakir Chowdhury.

I am especially indebted to Tony Kensington, of Aspirations Accountants, who have been supportive of my career goals and worked actively to provide me with business growth support to pursue these goals. Also, the inspiration and encouragement from such persons as Ben Bradford, of BB7 in Rochester, Kent and Professor Tunde Fasanya, of the Federal University of Technology, Minna, Nigeria cannot be overlooked.

I am grateful to all of those with whom I have had the pleasure to work with during this and other projects, for the numerous parts they have played.

"I hear, I forget, I see, I remember. I do, I understand" - Confucius

Preface

Human culture today, thrives on knowledge. It is manifested in the items we buy, the things we do, or in the activities we invest time on. Possessing and using knowledge effectively gives advantages in making the right decision or strategy to implement. The Internet distributes knowledge at split-second rates. Laptops, tablets and smart phones all bring knowledge to our fingertips. As the adage says, "knowledge is power", but the power of knowledge becomes insignificant, when not effectively managed.

Organizations have a wealth of knowledge accessible through the people they touch internally, such as their employees, and externally, such as customers. Organizations that allow knowledge to go unmanaged may be giving their competitors the upper hand in the market. The organization that is able to capture, store, and retrieve knowledge effectively is then capable of learning as an organization. A learning organization is one where employees are empowered to change and develop new methods, thoughts, and strategies that will advance the mission of their organization, which ultimately leads to innovation.

Knowledge Management is the establishment of a system that captures knowledge purposefully for incorporating into business strategies, policies, and practices at all levels of the company. This book will guide you on how to initiate a knowledge management program at work. When it comes to knowledge management, any organization is able to implement a strategy, as long as they have human as a resource. Wherever there are humans working together for same organizational objectives, there is knowledge to be harvested, stored, and dispensed as needed. Therefore, at this point we can say that knowledge is the key to power.

"Knowledge is power" - Sir Frances Bacon

Chapter One

_____

Understanding Knowledge Management

The words knowledge and management are two very broad concepts when separated. When the two words come together, it speaks of a concept that strives to organize information in a way that produces an advantage for an organization. While anyone would think that harnessing the knowledge of an organization is a positive thing to do, there are many who do not see the value of knowledge management, they may see this as a waste of time. This is true of many other disciplines like project management. Many see planning and assessing risk as time consuming, and even time wasting. Therefore, they do not support initiatives that bring this change. In all honesty, change is the real issue.

This book will give you the tools to present knowledge management to your organization in the most positive way in order to gain the right support for it, as well as be accepted and thrive in your organization. The more information you can share with your organization about knowledge management the more apt they are in accepting it. This chapter explains the principles, history, and application of knowledge management in the workplace. This will be the base on which we will build upon throughout the entire book.

What is Knowledge?

The word knowledge is often confused for information or data. The online version of the

Oxford dictionary defines knowledge: "information, and skills acquired through experience or education; the theoretical or practical understanding of a subject".

Later in the book, I will expatiate on what data and information is. Both terms are a part of knowledge. Data is raw content, which by itself has no meaning or value. When data is grouped together, it becomes information. For example, getting a temperature reading of the climate outside on one day is meaningless without other information to make a comparison.

Once a database is created, it becomes information because comparisons can now be made. In terms of knowledge management, knowledge is information that is in context, producing an actionable understanding.

Back to our temperature scenario, when the temperature information is placed in context with say agriculture, then knowledge is created. For example, knowing that if temperatures fall below a certain point in January they tend to last for about a week. Orange farmers in Swaziland, a Southern Africa nation, must determine if they are going to harvest early or take other precautions like heating the orchard. The decision will be based on how long oranges can withstand cold conditions at a certain temperature.

Organizations and companies hold and transfer data and information that can be placed into context allowing an actionable event or an understanding to occur.

What then is Knowledge Management?

Knowledge management is a program or system designed to create, capture, share and leverage knowledge towards the success of the organization. This is easier said than done because instituting a knowledge management program requires many changes and support at all levels of the organization. Furthermore, there are different forms of knowledge to contend with and understand.

Knowledge can be tacit or explicit, which requires different strategies to capture each type. Another challenge is to distill the practice of knowledge management into one neat concept.

The main aim of this book is to provide you with the specific understanding you need to take away a good conceptual framework of knowledge management. This way you can communicate and manage a knowledge management project with the tools provided for successful implementation.

A Brief History

The origins of knowledge management can be traced back to the late 1970s. Everett Rogers and Thomas Allen's work in information transfer laid the foundation to the concept of how knowledge is created, implemented, and integrated throughout an organization.

In the 1980s, knowledge became a focal point to increasing the competitive edge for companies. People like Senge and Sakaiya discussed the advantages of creating learning and knowledge based organization. The primary object during this time was improving business in general.

In the 1990s, knowledge management was introduced into mainstream business management publications. Authors like Tom Stewart, Ikujiro Nonaka, and Hirotaka Takeuchi brought formality to the managing of knowledge. In the mid 1990's, the Internet became the channel where knowledge management expanded greatly.

The history of knowledge management has many prominent theorists like Karl Wiig, Peter Drucker, and Paul Strassmann. From information technology to improving how an organization learns, knowledge management started in many areas of business. There is no one source of its history. Nonetheless, knowledge management has a history of producing the kind of change businesses desire in terms of improving the communication of knowledge in order to achieve successful outcomes.

Today, knowledge management has many applications and is useful in most disciplines within an organization.

Applications in the Workplace

Knowledge management can be applied to many areas of the organization. Remember that knowledge management is not only storing knowledge. The larger focus is on sharing. With this in mind, applying knowledge management in the workplace is nearly unlimited. Areas that can benefit from knowledge management are as follows:

- Corporate governance
- Staff training
- Operations
- Human resources

- Marketing
- Information technology
- Research and development

Applying knowledge management in any one of these areas will lead to improved communication and responsiveness to change. Here are some potential benefits to implementing knowledge management:

- Encourage innovation by allowing ideas to flow throughout the organization

- Improve customer experience by becoming more efficient in service

- Increase profits by capitalizing on opportunities because of faster product-to-market time

- Increase retention rate of employees because of recognition and reward for their valuable knowledge input

- Reduce cost through improved internal efficiencies

Case Study

Jamie wrestled with a big problem that he thought had no solution. Jamie had been given a complicated problem to solve, but had been left empty-handed when it came to how to solve it. Jane caught wind of his dilemma and offered to lend him her ear. Together, they deduced that crucial information had been hidden in plain sight. An idea popped into Jamie's head and suddenly they were off to the races. Jamie and Jane uncovered the facts and found the hidden solution to Jamie's once impossible to solve problem. Jamie now armed with a solution could conquer the problem and no longer felt like he'd been anchored down in a sea of puzzles too hard to solve.

"The soft stuff is always softer than the hard stuff" - Roger Enrico

Chapter Two

The "Dos and Don'ts" of Knowledge Management

There are many ways to implement knowledge management. The information available to you may be overwhelming. Understanding the types of knowledge and places to acquire it will reduce errors and increase efficiency in implementing your knowledge management project. In this chapter, you will learn about data, information, tacit and explicit modes of knowledge, and categories where knowledge converges.

Data, Information, and Knowledge

Earlier when we discussed the definition of knowledge, we learned that knowledge was composed of data and information. Here is a summary of each component:

• Data is bits of content in either text or numerical format. By itself, data has no meaning.

• A finance company could collect credit scores from all their approved applications. The individual credit score does not mean much by itself. Let see what information does.

• Information is data that is accumulated to allow comparison, grouping, and categorizing which enables the content viewer to determine what to do with the data group.

- The credit scores collected in the last example is accumulated and categorized into high, medium, and low risk according to the credit score number.

- Knowledge is taking the information and putting context around it, making it actionable.

- If the finance company is trying to meet a regulation on how many risky loans are permitted in the loan portfolio, they may calculate the percentage of high-risk loan to the total loans on the books. The results could guide the company on new strategies to reduce the number of risky loans or help them maximize the risk because the risky loans are more profitable.

Now that you have a basic idea of what data, information, and knowledge is, here is something to avoid. Do not try to categorize items into data, information, and knowledge. The context of the information is in the eye of the beholder. Trying to do this could end your project early. Instead, focus on the type of knowledge the content represents.

The Tacit Mode

Tacit knowledge is knowledge that is not easily documented. It is transferred silently through behaviours and experience. Here are some examples of tacit knowledge:

- Know-how
- Judgment
- Experience
- Insight
- Rules of thumb
- Skills

Tacit knowledge is difficult to communicate because it is very personal and subjective. The knowledge resides deep within the person who holds it. Tacit knowledge is influenced by beliefs, ideals, values, and mental modes.

This mode of knowledge is easily overlooked because capturing it requires unconventional methods. These methods will be discussed in a later chapter of the book. In the meantime, when planning your knowledge management project, remember that there is knowledge floating around that is being transferred through on-the-job experience.

The Explicit Mode

Explicit knowledge is easier to recognize and document. It is easily communicated, written down, transferred, stored and retrieved. Explicit knowledge could be the steps on how to drive a car. The explicit knowledge is outlined in a manual and easily followed because of its structure. This is the most common form of knowledge found in most organizations. You may find this information in the following areas:

- Databases
- Manuals
- Training content

However, having only explicit knowledge is not always desirable. For example, would you feel comfortable with some who only knew how to drive a car by studying a manual as opposed to someone who has been driving for 10 years? The choice is easy because there is value in the experience acquired in 10 years of driving experience. The experienced driver cannot explain all the details, but there is knowledge that the careful observer may pick up.

Understanding where these transfers of knowledge happen is essential to designing your knowledge management system.

Identifying Conversion Categories

Conversion categories are areas where knowledge is converted or exchanged. The best way to think of these conversion categories is using the tacit and explicit modes for both the type of knowledge and the type of behavior. Here are some examples:

• On-the-job training allows people to exchange tacit knowledge through tacit behaviors because it is transferred from one individual to another through observation. In this situation, norms are reinforced and new knowledge could be created depending on the person being trained.

• Another category is when someone expresses his or her ideas and thoughts. This is still tacit knowledge but it is coupled with explicit behavior like talking about it aloud to others.

• Explicit knowledge and explicit methods form more common conversion points like databases, e-mails, and manuals.

• Another conversion point occurs when someone takes explicit knowledge from a database or manual and creates new knowledge that they internalize (tacit).

Understanding conversion categories enables you to determine where these categories exist in your organization. Overlooking conversion categories could lead to gaps in your knowledge management system. Later, you will learn how to determine conversion categories in more detail by using a thorough approach involving the end user.

Case Study

George remained laser-focused on the project at hand. He had already cooked up a solution. Nelson had ideas of his own swimming in his head. George stood his ground because he believed his idea solved everything. Nelson stood with a sly smile and a light bulb seemed to appear right next to him, Nelson knew that if they created the perfect blend of both of their solutions that all sides of this rather peculiar problem could be dealt with head-on. George and Nelson agreed that two heads were better than one and they cooked up a better solution by pulling elements from each of their ideas. George and Nelson kept their heads in the game and were able to emerge from their problem-solving quest victorious. Together, they concocted the perfect combination of know-how and experience and got the job done.

"A person who graduated yesterday and stops studying today is uneducated tomorrow" - Anonymous

Chapter Three

_____

The Knowledge Management Life Cycle

Knowledge management is a cycle of identifying information that may or may not be useful knowledge, formatting it into usable knowledge, and integrating it into the organization. In this chapter, we shall review the basic phases in knowledge management lifecycle and how to use them within an organization. This information will help you communicate to those in your organization the components of knowledge management in a way that makes sense, creating more support for your project.

Understanding Episodes

Episodes of knowledge transfer come in many forms. Understanding that anytime a problem is realized or a new venture on the horizon, there is a good possibility that there is knowledge to capture. There are instances where episodes are planned. Here are some examples:

• A new product is being developed and rolled out

• Entering into a new market or territory

• Internal restructuring like a new division or enhancement of an existing department

• Implementing a new program like enterprise wide project management program

- Building a new facility

- Mergers, new partnerships, and take-over of another company

- Change in leadership at the top level like a new Chief Executive Officer

Some episodes may occur unexpectedly. For example:
- A recall of a defective product
- New government regulations
- Dramatic changes in the market

Here are a few ideas you can use to help deal with episodes whether planned or unplanned:

- What essential actions does the affected area have to take?

- What decisions people in the affected area must make to complete their job?

- What information is needed in order to make those decisions and complete their job?

- Is it explicit? Maybe is stored in a database.

- Is it tacit? Does this information have to come from a person?

Acquisition

The acquiring stage seeks to obtain information from both internal and external sources. It addresses tacit and explicit modes of knowledge and involves many techniques. Acquiring information or knowledge can be seen as two categories: capturing and creating.

Capturing is acquiring information or knowledge that already exists and requires little adjustments to make it valuable to the organization. It can be internal information that is floating around the organization or external information or knowledge from outsides sources.

Creation is taking existing information or knowledge and combining it with other internal knowledge or information to produce new knowledge the organization can deem actionable. There may be some analyzing involved to make the new knowledge actionable for the organization. Here is a brief list of tools and techniques that helps to acquire knowledge:

• Explicit information exists here and may be used in combination to form new knowledge, which may be internal or external

- Repositories with document information
- Filing systems
- Tacit information exists between people or experts and stored information, which may be internal and external
- Experts sharing their ideas
- Databases with information
- Internal tools for knowledge creation and capturing
- Interviewing employees
- Knowledge teams
- External tools for information or knowledge capturing
- Data mining data warehouses
- External expert opinion (i.e. consultant)

Once the knowledge is acquired, it must be organized so it can be easily integrated into the organization.

Knowledge

Remember that knowledge is information that is placed in context so that it becomes actionable. In order for this to happen, knowledge must be evaluated against the business goals and strategies. Knowledge that is deemed useful for the organization passes on through to the next cycle and integrated.

Evaluating information or knowledge requires comparison to the goals, vision, mission, and strategies of the organization. Failing to align the knowledge to these business strategies could render the knowledge management program ineffective. Here are some areas to consider when evaluating knowledge:

- What is the nature of your organization
- Organization vision
- Organization goals
- Strategy to achieve goals

- Current business environment
- Industry

Knowledge that is not ready for integration may be stored for later use. Here are some ways to evaluate knowledge for integration:

- Knowledge committees
- Knowledge forums
- KM software

Each of these tools would require representation from many areas of the organization. The goal here is to deem acquired information or knowledge useful to the organization. Not all knowledge acquired must be integrated. If this were the goal, the knowledge management system would become too burdensome and run the risk of not being used.

Integration

Integration is making knowledge known. There are several general methods to getting knowledge out throughout the organization. Here are several examples:

• Broadcasting: e-mails, announcements, newsletters, are some examples of integrating knowledge by broadcasting

• Searching: databases, portals, extranets, records, are examples of integrating knowledge by making it searchable

• Teaching: classroom, webinars, computer-based training, are examples of how training can help integrate knowledge throughout the organization

• Sharing: yellow page system, best practices system, community boards, are examples of how sharing knowledge helps to integrate it throughout your organization

The exact designs and process will depend on how your culture's view of these tools and their place in the organization. Other considerations revolve on costs. Later in the book, we will get a chance to discuss modest, cost effective ways of implementing knowledge management within your organization.

Now that we have a better understanding of the knowledge management cycle, let us review past and present models. This will help you determine if in fact, you already have a knowledge management system in place, but it needs a little updating.

Case Study

Mark jeered at the changes, his company has just done a turn around and changed the rules of the game. Karen cheered to hide the snide remarks that escaped mark's lips. Mark couldn't make heads or tails of what had happened. Karen offered to help explain that the tides were changing and tried to get mark to jump on board. Mark fumed with anger. Smoke bellowed from his ears as he marched out of the meeting. Karen tried to get him to listen to reason and employed every tactic she knew. Mark couldn't see straight and covered his ears to avoid the message. Mark's head nearly exploded before the message rang loud and clear. He realized that change didn't mean disaster and that all would be well after all. Karen breathed a sigh of relief, glad that the crisis had been averted.

"The single greatest challenge facing managers in the developed countries of the world is to raise the productivity of knowledge and service works" –
Peter F. Drucker

Chapter Four

The New Knowledge Management Paradigm

With the advent of information technology, knowledge management has evolved into a technological based program. Understanding what knowledge management is today requires review of what it was in the past. What and how it is applied is the overall goal of knowledge management. Understanding these concepts will allow you to understand the principles behind today's knowledge management model. This in turn, will allow you to be more knowledgeable about the program you are about to introduce to your organization and recognize if you already have a knowledge management system in place but is outdated.

Paradigms of the Past

Knowledge management does have a past and there are models out there that rely on knowledge collection and storage as the design for a knowledge management system. What resulted from this strategy is usually a query database that employees used to search for knowledge. This approach had drawbacks. Here are some:

• High maintenance of knowledge, because all knowledge was put into the system
• Stored knowledge became outdated
• Employees did not use the system because it was too vast
• It was a go-to system
• It was a static system

- High cost in labor and hardware maintenance
- Knowledge usually inputted by one person or team
- Only good for explicit knowledge

After a while, organizations did not see value in these types of knowledge management systems. Research an old-style knowledge management system that was previously used. Get lessons learned from those who were involved and incorporate this information in your newer knowledge management system proposal.

The New Paradigm

The new paradigm for knowledge management is vastly different from the past. Instead of focusing on data storage and retrieval, the focus is on connections and networks involving employees. There is storage, but this would be more for sharing documents and reference materials. Storage would not be the end-all-be-all system for knowledge management.

Here are some characteristics involving the new model of knowledge management:
- Focus on networking technology
- Learning environment fostered
- Knowledge pushed out instead of stored
- Information is evaluated before integrating
- Good for both explicit and tacit knowledge
- Employees can contribute to the knowledge management system

Notice the emphasis on connections being made instead of a hub for knowledge. This system does have its benefits. Here are some:
- Real-time knowledge available
- More tacit knowledge captured

- Employees are constantly learning
- Organizational culture more open
- Knowledge is free flowing and dynamic

The new paradigm takes advantage of new technologies like sharing programs, portals, intranets, etc.

Of course, no system is perfect and the next topic will discuss the implications of establishing a knowledge management system.

Implications and Applications

As you contemplate the introduction of knowledge management to your organization, you should consider the implications that applying knowledge management brings. If your organization is not used to sharing information and learning, this could become an obstacle to your knowledge management project. Here are some questions to think about when dealing with your culture:

• What value does your culture places on communication?

• What silos exist in your culture that could be a potential roadblock to your KM project?

• What level of support does senior management give to this initiative?

• What value does your organization place on knowledge?

• How well does your organization respond to change?

• What value does your organization place on learning?

Considering these questions will help you determine how open your organizational culture is to implementing a knowledge management programme.

Another consideration is the effect of technology on the organization. The new programs and communication tools present some issues to address in your project plan. It is not wise to make your knowledge management project a technology project.

Finally, you also have to consider who will be the agents for championing and managing the knowledge management program as it develops within your organization. Who will do what? Choosing the wrong people could doom your project because of association with the wrong people. Think globally. If you are not a project manager, you should consider having one on your project. They are trained to watch for these types of risks.

The Knowledge Management Endgame

The most important message you should convey about knowledge management is what it will do for the organization. Simply suggesting knowledge management on its own merits will not gain the support you need. You must remember that knowledge management involves the entire organization and the benefits should span the entire organization.

Therefore, you should clearly communicate the knowledge management end game. Your knowledge management project should address one or more of the following areas to help ground it to a more common business strategy:

- Change management
- Best practices
- Risk management

- Benchmarking
- Increasing efficiency
- Increased quality

Placing knowledge management initially on the back burner, and then on the front will take the focus off the knowledge management project itself and place it on the business strategies that get the interest of managers, creating more support for your project.

The goal of knowledge management is to connect employees to one another in an effort to facilitate information sharing in a way that promotes learning and new knowledge that will help the organization gain a competitive advantage through increased efficiency, quality, and innovation.

Clearly communicating this to your stakeholders will create a solid foundation for support and growth of your knowledge management project.

In the next chapter, you will get some more background knowledge on the various types of knowledge management principles, which will increase your vocabulary and credibility in this discipline.

Case Study

William struggled underneath the mountain of paperwork that had taken over his office. William needed a steamroller to move around. Ben noticed his co-worker buried under an outdated organizational process and offered to help William dig his way out. Ben told William that his tactics were relics of the past. He advised that William get organized with a nice desktop folder and use a digital calendar to keep his appointments for him. William liked his ancient practices. They were like an old friend and William didn't want to let go of the past. Ben explained that William lived in the dark ages while everyone around him thrived in the light of new technology and new strategies. The light seemed like a good idea and he agreed to give it a shot because it had to be better than drowning in his own process.

"Imagination is more important than knowledge" –
Albert Einstein

Chapter Five

Knowledge Management Models

We are delving into the origins and core principles of knowledge management in this chapter. There are models that have influenced knowledge management greatly over the years and these are worth understanding. Again, by having more background information on the principles of knowledge management, you will be able to influence those in your organization that may not know of the origins and the extent of the history in this discipline. Many times, projects are doomed when the stakeholders do not understand the product. Lack of information when attempting to create change will typically create resistance to the change. Let us increase your knowledge and ability to share it.

The Nonaka and Takeuchi Model (SECI)

Ikujiro Nonaka and Hirotaka Takeuchi model of knowledge creation describes a spiraling process of tacit knowledge and explicit knowledge. They give an illustration of how knowledge is converted through four patterns. Here are the four patterns:

• Socialization: tacit knowledge transfers through individual interaction (tacit). The interaction does not have to involve language. It can be observed. Capturing this type of knowledge involves direct interaction with employees.

- Externalization: the first part of this pattern, involves tacit knowledge, which is made explicit because of the expression of the knowledge through ideas, images, words, concepts, and visuals to others. The second part is the translation of the knowledge into understandable formats.

- Combination: takes explicit knowledge and is communicated systematically (explicit).

There are three basic phases to this pattern:
- Capturing knowledge from inside and outside the organization and internalizing it
- Disseminating the explicit knowledge through networks and systems
- Processing the explicit knowledge into a more usable format like documents, plans, and reports

• Internalization: is the individual taking explicit knowledge and internalizing it to become tacit knowledge once again.

The SECI model basically takes individual tacit knowledge and evolves it into explicit knowledge through the four patterns until it then finally reaches the individual again, changing the explicit knowledge back to tacit when the individual learns from it.

Wiig Model

Karl Wiig focused on six strategies to organizational knowledge management process.

1. Knowledge management as a business strategy: this places knowledge management as a strategy that spans the entire organization

2. Managing intellectual assets strategy: this is a focus on the existing knowledge that is

present within the organization and utilizing them or enhancing them fully

3. Personal knowledge asset responsibility strategy: this is a strategy that support employees to develop their skills and knowledge, sharing it with others

4. Knowledge creation strategy: focuses on creating new knowledge through research and development for shaping the future of the organization

5. Knowledge transfer strategy: this is sharing and transferring best practices in support of improving quality and efficiency throughout the organization

6. Customer-focused knowledge strategy: this strategy focuses on understanding customer needs and provide products and services that address those needs.

The Wiig model is highly favored because it does address the organization as a whole and includes business areas that are commonly found in most organizations.

Kakabadse Model

Kakabadse identified five models for knowledge management.

• Philosophy based model: focuses on the organization's view or philosophy of knowledge. A company that focuses on the importance of knowledge should ask the following questions.

• What do we not know that we know?

• What do we know that we don't know?

- Cognitive model: makes knowledge an asset and it should be managed and accounted as a part of normal business.
- Network model: here knowledge is seen as requiring collaboration through networks, allowing teams to use the knowledge for the betterment of the organization.

- Community of practice model: takes knowledge and communicates it in a more relaxed and communal environment utilizing storytelling or metaphors as the channel. It is meant to breakdown complex knowledge into a simple format.

- Quantum model: it positions knowledge as scenario-driven instead of fact-driven. This model makes knowledge dynamic and adjustable to the scenario instead of referring to the knowledge as a static fact, leaving little room for innovation.

Boisot Model

Boisot describes a knowledge management model that is three-dimensional. His Information Space or I-Space philosophy describes three axes.

1. Uncodified to codified
2. Concrete to abstract
3. Undiffused to diffused

Boisot then describes a Social Learning Cycle that works within the I-Space model. This process flows through six phases:

• Scanning involves knowledge obtained from the environment, which is uncodified.

• Codification knowledge is given structure through problems being solved with that knowledge.

- Abstraction is when new and codified knowledge is applied to a wide range of scenarios, making this knowledge more abstract in nature.
- Diffusion is when knowledge is shared with the population.

- Absorption is when the knowledge is applied to many scenarios, which produces new individual learning, which becomes uncodified because it returns to tacit knowledge.

- Impacting is when the abstract knowledge is integrated into organizational practices as rules, policies, and procedures.

By now, you may feel a bit overwhelmed by this information. Remember this information was presented so you can have a base knowledge of several of the principles that contributed to knowledge management, as we know it today. Do not worry about getting all the details.

Case Study

Paula marched over to the computer and typed without saying a word. Rhonda quirked up her eyebrow, confusion written on her face. Paula had been told to train Rhonda. Rhonda stood behind Paula and watched her fire away at the keys as she entered all of the necessary information. As if on cue, Paula typed with one hand and jotted down notes with the other. Paula tossed the note over her shoulder to Rhonda and on it were the step-by-step directions for the new process. Rhonda wanted to thank Paula, but Paula continued working at a feverish pace until the entire information had been loaded. In the blink of an eye, Paula had completed the task and walked away without uttering a word. Rhonda remained confused about Paula's coaching style, but found that she'd learned a lot by watching Paula perform the duties and having ample notes to boot.

"Companies have a hard time distinguishing between the cost of paying people and the value of investing in them" - *Thomas A. Stewart*

Chapter Six

Building A Knowledge Management Rationale

All projects must a have a reason for its existence, therefore the implementation of a knowledge management program is no different. A good rationale for implementing knowledge management will help influence those that control budgets to see the value of sinking funds into your project. This chapter will discuss in simple manner how you can develop a solid rationale for implementing knowledge management in an organization, by building a business case, sharing success stories, and making the knowledge in your organization valuable by turning it into a commodity.

Why Rationale is Necessary

Simply saying the organization needs knowledge management is not going to get you the support you need to implement this project. You need a rationale or reason for implementing knowledge management. Another mistake you want to avoid is focusing only on the return on investment for implementing knowledge management. There are more interesting reasons to implement knowledge management and you will need to point that out.

Below are some reasons to implement knowledge management. However, you will have to evaluate each to determine if this will be seen as a viable reason to implement:

- Creating a culture that shares knowledge
- Using knowledge management to enhance your customers' experience

- Creating a learning environment
- Improve company performance
- Help to resolve an identified gap in the business

These are just a few reasons. The idea is to take the attention off knowledge management and placing on a business need or driver. This will get the attention of top management and maybe open the door to a project sponsored from the top level, which is a good thing. Developing your rationale may be the most important part of your proposal. Take the time to research and determine what your company values.

Building a Business Case

Building a business case goes beyond the rationale we discussed earlier. A business case outlines the business reasons that justify implementing knowledge management. The business case outlines the benefits of implementing the program and the potential consequences of not using knowledge management.

This does not have to be complicated. In fact, I suggest three basic steps you can use to make your business case.

• Make knowledge an asset to the organization. There is a cost to knowledge. If you are able to point out that fact to the organization, they may realize that they may be losing knowledge. Here are some areas to discuss in your business case:

• Market value: place a value certain knowledge assets like databases, networks, team of experts. Provide some benchmarking numbers to demonstrate the value.

• Cost: put a cost figure on how much it takes to train a new employee or what it took to develop a current asset like your organization's intranet.

• Replacement: do a "what-if" scenario of lost knowledge and the cost to replace it.

• Liability: show potential liability due to regulation or contract violation because of poorly managed knowledge.

• Make knowledge management a benefit to the bottom line. Discuss how knowledge management can increase productivity, time-to-market for new products, and customer service. Here are specific areas you can emphasize:

• Knowledge: having information at the employee's fingertips gives them access to expert information, allowing them to take action quicker.

• Intermediate: discuss reduction in duplicate of efforts and faster new hire adaptation.

• Organizational: show the cost reduction, increased productivity, and potential in innovations.

• Customer and stakeholders: discuss product improvements, better quality service, and increased value.

• Demonstrate knowledge management as a cost-effective tool. This is best for organizations that are cost conscious, as most organisation would. Your focus here is on saving money through knowledge management by sharing best practices and focusing activities that bring in the most revenue.

Finding Success Stories

Incorporating success stories into your knowledge management case will help to demonstrate the value through an objective source. You will have to perform some research and find credible sources that demonstrate success when implementing knowledge management. Avoid presenting your entire research work. Instead provide an executive summary with bullet points. Here are some areas where you can find research on knowledge management successes:

- Research the web for white papers or reports

- Obtain an industry journal or magazine

- Go to the library and read books on knowledge management

Here are two companies that have successful knowledge management programs you may want to research:

- Hewlett-Packard
- British Petroleum (BP)

The Commoditization / Customization Model

Knowledge management is not a one-size fits all programme. No organization wants to be pitched a bland and generic knowledge management programme. If you want commitment to this program, you will have to customize your knowledge management programme. A vision of what this program will look like once it is implemented will get you more support for this project. Presenting a generic program will be subject to criticism and may be rejected.

Here are easy ways to begin customizing your project. Determine what your area of concentration is, the two general areas worth considering are:

1. Do you want to connect people?
2. Do you want to document knowledge?

The type of work and level of collaboration needed will help you determine which area you want to work with.

Here are some factors for wanting to connect people:
- Work performed is complex and requires expert judgment or interpretation
- Work requires a high level of interdependence
- Knowledge is largely tacit

Here are some factors for wanting to document knowledge:
- Work performed is routine
- Work is performed with little or no interdependency
- Knowledge is mostly explicit

Once you determine the area of concentration, you are then able to define what the system will look like. If it is connecting people, your vision will be networks, and programs that support this strategy. If it is documenting knowledge, then your vision will outline databases and retrieval systems. The more detailed you are, the more this becomes customized. The goal is to make knowledge management a commodity within your organization, creating a desire to own it.

Case Study

Tom held his hands in the air because the ship had sunk. Tom didn't know which way to go and could only watch the implosion that inevitably would happen if his coworkers didn't get on the same page. Tom watched money fly out the door every day and with little time left on the clock, he panicked about what the consequences would be. Tom couldn't see a light at the end of the tunnel. He'd ridden the gravy train for too long and never got around to implementing an accounting process that would keep the business afloat. He felt like he'd drowned in debt and worry and landed in the sea without a paddle. Caroline threw him a life vest and helped him make small changes that could yield big results. Together, they were able to trudge through the mess and work toward a solution.

"There is less fear from outside than from inside inefficiency, miscalculation, lack of knowledge..." - Anonymous

Chapter Seven

Customizing Knowledge Management Definitions

At this point, you want to customize what knowledge management will look like within your organization. This is important because your project stakeholders would like to know what you are attempting to achieve. Without a clear definition of what knowledge management will be in your organization, you may lose support for your project, and support is key.

In this chapter, you will learn how to define your knowledge management project by identifying the components, customizing them to suit your organization in a body of knowledge.

Components of a Knowledge Management Definition

Having a good foundation in project management will help you to define your project and communicate clearly to stakeholders. If you do not possess project management skills, you may want to get someone that does on your team. Remember that implementing knowledge management has to be a team effort in order for it to permeate throughout your organization.

Defining your knowledge management program involves discussion around the following items:

• Provide a concise description of deliverables, tasks, or action items. This should explain any new systems, processes, policies, and specifications of results you are planning to achieve. The more detail the better. Each deliverable should have an owner responsible for completing the task along with a proposed date of completion.

• In your definition, you should include the benefits to implementing knowledge management. This was discussed earlier this workshop. This is probably the best place to put this information since this document will be the one used to gain approval for your project.

• Develop a list of objectives. Remember to link the objective to business drivers and organizational needs. Avoid making knowledge management itself as the main objective. Tie it to performance, organizational efficiency, etc.

• Define what kind of support is needed from the organization. You will need support from other departments like IT, training, and marketing. Make sure you speak with those areas first to ensure they are on board before you list them as a support group. Remember support means that they are willing to lend you resources from their area to help with your project.

• Discuss changes to any business processes. Then you should list new processes or areas that will be created because of implementing knowledge management. Perhaps you are proposing a new position that manages knowledge management such as a Chief Knowledge Officer (CKO). Define that role here as a part of the total knowledge management definition.

• Provide a timeline of events that maps the progress of this project. You can focus on milestones instead of the details.

Defining your knowledge management program will give your management team something to reference, making it easier for them to render a decision. Your goal is to win them over to knowledge management. Clear definition will help you achieve this.

Customizing the Components

To customize your knowledge management program to fit the organization, you will have to involve the organization. You could spend months putting a program together only to find out that the employees do not like the system.

Customizing will involve a few crucial steps. At first, these steps may seem like a lot of trouble to perform, but in the end, it will reap rewards that will benefit your knowledge management project.

Here are some steps you can take to customize your program:

• Involve the employees or users of the knowledge management system. Hold focus groups, surveys, and one-on-one meetings to gather information on system expectations, desired features, type of knowledge they value, and potential drawbacks to your plans. All of this planning and preparation should help to avoid costly mistakes.

• Involve management in your customization process. Get valuable insight to strategic goals. Have them poke holes in your plan. Allowing them to give input and advice will make them part owner of this program, allowing you to get more details that will help you tailor your knowledge management program to the organization.

When in the process of customizing your program, remember to remain objective and open to feedback. If people start to get the feeling that you are sensitive to feedback, they may avoid giving you feedback.

Finally, remember to take into account your organizational culture. If they are not used to being open to sharing information, you may have to come up with a subtler approach to sharing information. Always keep in mind what the culture values and incorporate that somehow.

Take the time to do research on this topic. This book gives you the basics so you can have a better understanding of the knowledge management concept. Use the web, read books or research companies that use knowledge management. When you do your homework, you will expand how you can customize knowledge management to meet your organization's needs.

Creating a KMBOK

A knowledge management body of knowledge or KMBOK is an enterprise wide program that captures all knowledge within the organization. The actual knowledge management system oversees all major areas of knowledge within the organization. There are three major areas in developing a KMBOK.

- Project management is how the organization manages the temporary activities within the organization. Many companies use a well-known body of knowledge for this discipline published by the Project Management Institution aptly names the Project Management Body of Knowledge or PMBOK.

- Leadership and managerial knowledge is how the management in an organization operates. This involves their strategic leadership skills, managerial skills, their roles within the organization, and their functions.

- Organizational structure knowledge involves all the systems and processes that define the company. Organizational factors like the culture, the people, and the processes and the way the organization handles challenges make up this area of knowledge.

Remember that above these three broad categories exists your knowledge management program, which threads all of this knowledge into a network for sharing across the organization.

Creating the KMBOK is not a requirement to implementing knowledge management. However, as your knowledge programme matures, you may want to develop a KMBOK so the organization has an understanding of what all is involved in the daily operations as it relates to knowledge.

Case Study

Anne and will scurried about like two pieces of a puzzle that had no home. Changes had been made and both Anne and will had not yet found their place. Anne nudged and budged her way through tasks, hoping that she'd made the right decision. Will clobbered about as if he had no care in the world. Will figured he'd worry about it later. Anne continued to fret and beads of sweat formed on her forehead. Will ran haphazardly through his day. Neither made any progress and neither went in search of answers. Their supervisor noticed the mayhem and had an "a-ha moment". Anne and will needed a road map for success and that would calm the storm before the clock ran out on both of them.

"People don't resist change. They resist being changed!" - Peter M. Senge

Chapter Eight

Implementing Knowledge Management in Your Organization

Now you are ready to put together your project plan. Like in any other project, there is a level of support both politically and financially. The more organized and detailed your plan is, the more your chances of support increases. Management rarely supports poorly planned projects, especially in tight budget situations. In this chapter, you will learn how to gather support, find funding for your project, map a plan, and implement your project in the case where there is no budget available for your project.

Gathering Support

In all honesty, it is best to gain support from a senior level or executive manager. You may be able to begin a grassroots campaign for your knowledge management project, but without the right level of support from senior management, you may find yourself fighting an uphill battle. Here are some advantages to gaining senior-level support.

• You are in a better position to get funding for your project. Usually senior management approves project budgets and the resources dedicated to them.

• You gain valuable insight to the world of senior management.

• You may learn how to communicate at a strategic level. Remember that your knowledge management project is for the entire organization. Having a narrow scope could lead to missed opportunities for more support.

• A senior manager gives more credibility to your project and a voice at the higher levels of the organization.

Getting a senior level manager to sponsor your project is not always easy to do. You must pitch your project to the seniors and hope that one expresses interest. Even when this happens, you will have to cultivate the relationship. They may not want to move that fast. They must think about other important issues. Adding one more may not be a desired outcome of their relationship with you.

Another way to build support for your project is to invite those to your project team who may have differing opinions than you do. Do not be discouraged by those who do not always agree with you. Having everyone on the project team think like you may lead to slow development of the program. When there is healthy debate, innovative ideas emerge, shaping your project.

If you welcome diversity and maintain a focus on involving someone from the senior management level, you will begin to build the support you need to implement knowledge management in your organization.

Identifying Opportunities for Revenue Streams

The best chances of getting funding for your projects rely heavily on how well you present the budget. Once again, good project management and budgeting skills will help, and if you do not have the skills to build a budget, get help from someone who knows.

Next, you want to determine what type of organization you have. If your organization is centralized, meaning there is a strong governing body over all the departments, and then you will want to approach that team to ask for funds. If your organization is de-centralized, meaning there is weak governing body, and the departments are autonomous, you may want to find a department that is open to funding your project. For instance, IT, HR or R&D are good departments to ask for help.

Become familiar with how your organization handles budgeting. Some companies do budgets once a year and that is it until next year. You will have to time your project for this event. Other have more flexible budgets and you may tap into some reserves, but you must gain the support from someone in senior leadership so they can get you access to those funds.

Your overall budget approach should offer various pricing points. Presenting one big budget makes it easier to say no. Instead, offer various scenarios with different cost structures. When you offer a variety of cost options, senior management may be more incline to approve one of your proposals.

Try not to low-ball your budget either just to get it approved. Underfunding could lead to project failure. Consider all the cost involved with launching a knowledge management project. Here are some items to think about, which you may need to include in your budget:

- Ongoing development of project team
- Training and learning costs
- Memberships to knowledge management organizations
- Consultant costs
- Funds to use to keep the project team's morale going

Knowledge management could be a costly venture, but if you present a detailed budget with various pricing points and present that to the right group and the right time you may get the funding you need to implement you project.

Key Knowledge Management Techniques
There are many knowledge management techniques. We are going to learn a few according to each of the major phases of the knowledge management cycle. First, the

phases to knowledge management are as follows:

- Knowledge creation
- Knowledge capturing
- Knowledge codification
- Knowledge integrations and sharing

Here are some techniques for each of the phases mentioned:

- Creation

☐ Team dedicated to combining new knowledge with existing knowledge to create updated knowledge for sharing

☐ Job analysis where a job is broken down into the details and knowledge is created by studying task and task order

- Capturing

☐ Tacit knowledge

o Expert evaluation

- o Interviewing
- ☐ Explicit knowledge
- o Observation
- o Brainstorming
- o Concept mapping

- • Codification: remember that codification is converting tacit knowledge into explicit knowledge. Explicit knowledge is codified by organizing it, categorizing it, and indexed.
- ☐ Knowledge maps
- ☐ Decision table
- ☐ Decision tree

- • Integration and sharing
- ☐ Portals
- o Collaboration
- o Content manager
- ☐ E-world
- o Intranet

- o Extranet
- o Groupware
- ☐ E-business
- o Supply chain management
- o Customer relationship management
- ☐ Learning
- o Traditional
- o Web-based

There is an array of tools to use when practicing knowledge management. Researching best practices with organizations with a similar structure to your organization is helpful in developing your plan. There are also packaged programs that offer a suite of solutions that can meet many of these needs. Leveraging your IT department is also a good thing to do especially with the selection of programs for your knowledge management system. They will give you details on how the program integrates with the company's system. In addition, you will want to identify who will maintain such systems. Many programs are installed by IT, but managed by users throughout the organization.

A Map for Success

Here is a map for successful rollout of your knowledge management project.

- Vision

o Creating a vision of what the organization will look like with a knowledge management system will have your leaders and users see the future and the need to invest in such a program. Describe to them what this will look like when it is done.

- Timeline

o Make sure you plan accurate and realistic timelines. A decent knowledge management program takes years to develop. Making this a quick fix project will not get you the seriousness you need from your stakeholders. Use milestones to communicate your timeline.

- Strong leadership

o Know that you will be challenged, face opposition to change, and will have to work around it.

- Strategy

o Use a small approach. Implement small project instead of one large one.

- Internal marketing

o Develop a shared definition of knowledge management. Get with those who have influence and hold discussions. Try to avoid telling them what it is. Get their input and incorporate it into the message.

o Develop a quick 30-second ad for your project. Think of creative ways to discuss knowledge management without overbearing everyone with diagrams and charts. Avoid these tools. Instead, develop a clear, crisp pitch that describes the vision.

o Get your marketing department involved.

- Focus on business results

o Tie what knowledge management will do for the business

- Multiple pricing points

o Develop different budget costs

- Development of a prototype and run a test pilot

o Start small and develop a prototype and hold pilot test before full rollout

The No-Budget Scenario

If you run into a no-budget situation with your project, there is still some frugal ways to implement a knowledge management program. It may not be fancy, but it gets the ball rolling until there is a budget. Here are some things you can use to help you manage knowledge.

• First, take inventory of any tools that currently exist that you can leverage and make feasible with slight adjustments. See if you have the following:

o E-mail

o Intranet

o Web portal

o Electronic conferencing tools

o Databases

o Chat capabilities

- Second, get with your IT department and see if you can make some modifications to any of the tools mentioned above.

o Create an e-mail group

o Create an internal intranet page

o Create some type of collaborative site on using the web portal

o Network using existing conferencing tools

o Use the existing database technology to create a separate database (ex. Microsoft Access)

The only expense you may incur is labor. If your organization desires knowledge management, but does not have the monetary resources to support it, negotiate resources that could help make enhancements to existing programs and systems. You may need to develop guidelines and policies so this can be trained to staff.

Case Study

Josh looked like his head might explode. He'd just heard the solution, but that left him juggling more questions than answers. Norman spoke a mile a minute. Stars danced in his eyes. Norman thought his idea to be superior. Josh couldn't see straight. The solution felt like a winding road. He needed to figure out a way to shorten the route. Norman refused to budge. Josh walked Norman through the very long process to prove that something had to give. Norman realized his solution felt more like a train wreck and agreed to let Josh lead the way. Josh's plan cut out the middle-man and made great strides in improving their process efficiently and without giant hoops to jump through. Norman learned a hard lesson, but in the end, celebrated Josh's courage to challenge his idea and lead their team to victory on a not-so-winding road.

*"A manager is responsible for the application
of knowledge" –
Peter F. Drucker*

Chapter Nine

Tips for Success

You need all the help you can get when trying to create a change as great as the one involved with implementing knowledge management within your organization. Items that help to increase success may include a person in charge of knowledge management at you organization. This is just one example. In this chapter, you will learn the tips to successful implementation of knowledge management at the workplace.

About the Chief Knowledge Officer

Giving someone a fulltime job in knowledge management is a definite advantage. If your company is serious about knowledge management, they may like the idea of a Chief Knowledge Officer (CKO). CKOs will keep knowledge management in the forefront of the business. They are in touch with the business strategies on a day-to-day basis. The role of a CKO in the industry is not clearly defined so their role may change from company to company.

The role of a CKO can be temporary until the knowledge management is fully in place. Remember that this could take several years to achieve. Their role may be permanent and oversee areas like learning and education.

If the organization decides to hire from the outside, the new CKO will have the knowledge about systems, but will not have the cultural understanding, increasing implementation time of the knowledge management project. Internal promotions to CKO address the cultural aspect and can exploit established connections with senior management. On the other hand, being internal could leave the CKO blinded by culture and unable to see their faults.

Hiring an external resource and pairing them with an internal employee could resolve this problem and move the project forward. Of course, they would have to get along well.

Here is a quick list of what a CKO does:
• Identify gaps
• Benchmark performance standards
• Integrate need throughout the organization
• Manage resources from various areas within organization

- Develop strategies
- Build support
- Collaborate
- Leverage strengths within the current culture
- Create sharing and learning environment
- Practice change management
- Demonstrate results
- Recognize and champion success

Knowledge Management Skill Checklist

Here is a brief list of skills needed to manage a knowledge management project.

- Must have a passion for knowledge management
- Must be able to constantly share the message of knowledge management
- Must have an entrepreneurial spirit and own the program
- Self-starter

- Risk taking
- Create new capabilities
- Change the way people think
- Change the way people work
- Must be able to persuade
- Excellent written and verbal skills
- Must be IT savvy

These skills apply to whoever is leading the knowledge management project. These skills are critical to the success of the project.

The Knowledge Management Imperative
Presenting a plan or strategy without any energy or reason for change may get your project on the stove but on the backburner. There must be a healthy level of urgency to getting this project underway. Here are a couple of steps you can take to create a burning platform.

- Get your stakeholders to a healthy level of survival anxiety. Avoid over dramatizing the point as you may raise skepticism. Present information and facts that point to a choice that must be made. Let them come to their own conclusion. Here is an example:
- If we continue this path we will lose X amount of dollars.
- Make knowledge management the choice for a solution. Here is an example:
- If we go with knowledge management, we will increase profits by X percent.

In any case, the burning platform formula is this:

- Present the realistic dilemma
- Provide facts and figures
- Present the choices
- Pause and let them think it about it
- Be prepared to answer questions

The Hype Curve

The hype cycle consists of five phases.

• Trigger phase is when something new is introduced, it creates a buzz, and there is a high level of interest in the item.

• Peak of expectations is when the hype is build up to the point where the employees will start generating unrealistic expectations.

• Trough of disillusionment is when the employees are disappointed because the item did not meet their inflated expectations.

• Slope of enlightenment is when employees experiment with the item and understand the benefits and practicality of the item.

• Plateau of productivity is when the benefits of the item are generally accepted. The item stabilizes and is ready for enhancements and evolution.

Understanding these phases will help to manage the unrealistic peaks and the depths of the trough. Here are some things to think of when marketing your knowledge management project.

- Avoid sensationalizing it or making big promises you cannot keep.
- Set expectations ahead of time. Let them know this will be a work in progress and will take time to perfect.
- Communicate often and collect feedback.
- Publish the benefits to help push the employees to the plateau phase

Barriers and Helpers to Success

The biggest challenge you will face is the culture. If your culture is open to change and embrace learning and sharing this will help you move your project along. On the other hand, if your culture is closed and resistant to change, you will find it challenging to implement your project. Here are some things to consider as you navigate your culture and change:

• Organizational culture is tacit and deeply rooted
• Culture is not easily changed
• Culture is complex and difficult to define
• Analyze your culture and determine the tolerance for change
• Defining knowledge management could be a challenge in certain cultures

Here are some ways to overcome those barriers and achieve success.

• Learn to understand your culture and work within it
• Review the organization's history from a member's point of view

- Listen to the stories told within the organization. This will give you a sense of what the culture tends to assume
- Approach middle management. They are the gate to the general employee population
- Create a reward system for knowledge management
- Champion success stories throughout the organization
- View change as three stages
- Current, transition, and future state
- Develop a plan for the transition state and cater to how the organization adopts to change
- Provide training early in the change process

Case Study

Joanna had too much on her plate. Her to-do list had grown a mile a minute. Joanna needed help to implement the new changes. Michael saw her struggle and offered to lighten her load. "What do you need?" He asked. Joanna gave him the condensed version of her dilemma. Michael nearly toppled over at the sound of her words. Michael had an 'aha moment' and drew out a plan that would save the day. Michael declared that they needed reinforcements. Joanna and Michael gathered their personal army of coworkers. Michael laid out the plan. Joanna watched all the pieces come in place. A complete change had been made in no time flat. Michael and Joanna had accomplished their mission and crossed the finish line with coworkers at their sides.

"The organization cannot create knowledge on its own without the initiative of the individual and the interaction that takes place within the group" –
Nonaka & Takeuchi

Chapter Ten

Advance Topics

This chapter will discuss some advance concepts related to knowledge management. These concepts will help you understand when knowledge management becomes a mature program in your organization. In addition, you will learn how to keep it healthy and strong throughout the years after it has been implemented.

The Knowledge Management Maturity Model

The KM maturity model describes five levels.

- Initial: the organization is at the beginning and just starting out in tracking their performance using knowledge management
- Respectable: the organization is experiencing success, but problem areas exist.
- Defined: the organization is being managed well; it is competing strongly within the market.
- Managed: the organization is in control of the market and employees are empowered to make decisions.
- Optimizing: the organization is at a mature level and has a strong reputation, and is setting trends in the market.

This model will help you understand where you are in the process. Remember that it could take years for knowledge management to affect your organization in the way level 5 describes.

Absorptive Capacity

The absorptive capacity is the organization's ability to recognize the value of new knowledge, integrate it, and apply it in a way that creates competitive advantage. The ability for an organization to do this depends on the prior knowledge and diversity of background.

There are two levels of capacity:

• Potential Capacity is the organization's receptiveness to acquiring and assimilating external knowledge.

• Realized Capacity is the organization's ability to combine existing knowledge and new knowledge and integrating it.

There are indicators in determining the extent of absorptive capacity.

• Level of knowledge acquisition

- How much is invested in research and development
- Assimilation
- Number of references to other sources in an organization's publication
- Transformation
- Number of new products ideas
- Exploitation
- Number of new product rollouts

Rustiness

Here are some tips to keeping your knowledge management project vibrant over time.

- Do not rely on IT to sustain your program. Knowledge management is not a program. It is a philosophy and culture. Keep involved in the process and always look to new ways of doing things or improvements.

- Expand your support to as many high-level managers. Do not rely on one sponsor. What will you do if they leave the organization?
- Keep training employees on new technologies and processes.
- Keep the lines of communication open.
- Work to make knowledge management a standard in the organization
- When possible, build your KMBOK

Process Model Types

A process model describes how a process should be done. It outlines what the process looks like. It is usually an illustration, which conveys the actions, relationships, and reasons to completing a process. Using a process model will help to make the process more memorable to your organization. You can use many models. Once you finalize what the process for knowledge management will look like, it is a good step to put it in a process model.

The example you received is just one way to put your knowledge management program in an illustration. There are many ways to achieve this. The point here it to create a process model to help solidify knowledge management and create a lasting image for your organization.

Case Study

Tony had beads of sweat swimming on his forehead. Amanda watched and ran to his aid. Tony explained that the work day felt like an uphill battle for him. Amanda knew just what to do. Amanda volunteered to help get him over the hump one step at a time. Together, they able to dig through the pile of work weighing tony down and chip away part of his problem. Tony couldn't believe how much lighter he felt in no time flat. Amanda beamed with pride. Amanda knew that climbing a hill with no support didn't make any sense at all. Tony learned a hard lesson. Amanda hit the nail on the head. Tony needed to have the proper tools in place to make any headway in his day. Amanda opened his eyes to a much more efficient way of getting the job done.

"Wisdom is not a product of schooling but the lifelong attempt to acquire it" - Albert Einstein

Final Thoughts – Some Words of Wisdom

• *The store of wisdom does not consist of hard coins, which keep their shape as they pass from hand to hand; it consists of ideas and doctrines whose meanings change with the minds that entertain them* - **John Placentas**

• *Of central importance is the changing nature of competitive advantage - not based on market position, size and power as in times past, but on the incorporation of knowledge into all of an organization's activities* - **Leif Edvinsson**

• *Innovations are created primarily by investment in intangibles. When such investments are commercially successful, and are protected by patents or first-mover advantages, they are transformed into tangible assets creating corporate value and growth* - **Baruch Lev**

ABOUT THE AUTHOR

Nicholas has over 18 years proven expertise in development and management of training; especially in sustainable development, general management and construction / health and safety. He has background in a wide range of industries, including construction, agriculture, corporate management, hygiene services and occupational health and safety.

He was instrumental to the coordination of extension workers and service providers training for over 7 years at Farmers Care Project in Swaziland, Southern Africa from 1999, where he remains an ex-officio director to date. He is the Executive Director at the Centre for Regional and International Development, and was instrumental to CRID's extended operations in the African sub region, and has played key roles in its extension to Asia and the Caribbean.

Nicholas has a MA in Development Studies (work in progress). He also has a B. Agric with specialty in Animal Sciences.

He is married and a father of four children.

Services

Please be aware that I am happy to help if:
You wish to utilise this information for staff training and development, including:

- Provision of trainer's manual.
- Provision of delegate's handbook.
- Provision of PowerPoint presentation.
- Provision of case study and exercises handouts.
- Provision of training event on the topic or developing your trainers to utilise materials provided.

Your organisation wishes to set up a knowledge management unit (KMU), including:

✓ Set-up and initial consultations
✓ Consultancy work to implement

- ✓ Support towards evaluation and monitoring of KMU
- ✓ Developing your own personalise KM book of knowledge

Any other support you may require utilising this material corporately.

For any (or all) of the above, contact me.

Email: nicholas.a@crid.co.uk

Website: www.crid.co.uk

Unit 3, Epsilon House, Laser Quay, Culpeper Close, Medway City Estate, Kent, ME2 4HU, United Kingdom.

10411 Motor City Drive, Suite 750, 7th Floor, Bethesda, MD 20817, United States.

PASSIONATE ABOUT BOOKS

Peaches Publications have over a decade of experience, knowledge and information in the book publishing industry. Many authors are duped into spending thousands of pounds to bring their books to market. We use our cost-effective formula to help you go to print for the fraction of the price.

We help new authors bring their books to life by providing top quality services:

Digital publishing	Book publishing
Content	Amazon
Editing	Framework of books
Proof reading	Marketing
Book printing	Research
Sales	Print on demand
Kindle	Book coaching
Copyright	

www.peachespublications.com

Useful Links

Some helpful site for Knowledge Management

https://www.brainyquote.com/quotes/topics/topic_knowledge.html

http://www.knowledge-management-tools.net/KM-best-practices.html

https://www.forbes.com/sites/lisaquast/2012/08/20/why-knowledge-management-is-important-to-the-success-of-your-company/#6deb8df33681

http://crid.co.uk/site/Downloads/CRID%20-%20Programme%20Information%202016.pdf

Some other helpful books on Knowledge Management:

Knowledge Management in Organizations: A Critical Introduction; by Donald Hislop

The Knowledge Manager's Handbook: A Step-by-Step Guide to Embedding Effective Knowledge Management in your Organization; by Nick Milton and Patrick Lambe

Harvard Business Review on Knowledge Management: The Definitive Resource for Professionals; by Harvard Business Review

Records Management and Knowledge Mobilisation: A Handbook for Regulation, Innovation and Transformation; by Stephen Harries

Study Notes

....

....

....

....

....

....

....

....

....

....

....

....

....

....

....

....

....

....

Study Notes

....

....

....

....

....

....

....

....

....

....

....

....

....

....

Study Notes

....

....

....

....

....

....

....

....

....

....

....

....

....

....

Study Notes

....

....

....

....

....

....

....

....

....

....

....

....

....

....

Knowledge Management